All

Names
Names f...

GW01466069

Editorial Board

Madhvi Kapur
Neeta Datta
Sharmistha Dash

New Dawn

NEW DAWN
a division of Sterling Publishers (P) Ltd.
A-59, Okhla Industrial Area, Phase-II, New Delhi-110020
Tel : 6313023, 6320118, 6916209, 6916165
E-mail : ghai@nde.vsnl.net.in
www.sterlingpublishers.com

All You Wanted to Know About - Baby Names
© 2000, Sterling Publishers Private Limited
ISBN 81 207 2298 1
Reprint 2001

Published by Sterling Publishers Pvt. Ltd., New Delhi-110020.
Lasertypeset by Vikas Compographics, New Delhi-110020.
Printed at Prolific Incorporated, New Delhi-110020.

Contents

CASTLE VALE

Preface

Everyone has a name. A name gives a person an identity. In most countries, people have at least two names, a name that a child has been given, and a family name. The family name is also called a surname or last name which is common to all family members. The surname is derived either from the village or tribe the family belongs to or from the kind of work they do for a livelihood.

The given name is the one that distinguishes the child from other family members.

A girl child is usually named after birds, flowers, deities or the softer qualities of a woman. A boy child is usually named after qualities of valour, honour, bravery, or joy.

With the arrival of a new born, the parents are faced with the problem of naming a child. All parents wish to give their child a name which is meaningful and at the same time exclusive.

Most of the names have more than one meaning. This comprehensive collection comprises both religious and general names.

Nationality	If parents select a foreign sounding name it should not be unpronounceable or unspellable.
Religion	Religion plays an important role in an Indian's life. Most of our names have some religious connotation, or belong to gods and goddesses.
Gender	In Sikh names, there is hardly any gender difference. The difference is apparent only when the suffix 'Singh' (for males) and 'Kaur' (for females) is added to the first name.
Number	Many Indian communities follow the trend of adding the grandparents', parents' name before the child's name. The parents should give this a serious thought before burdening their child with a long name.
Pronunciation	Parents should choose a name that has a clear pronunciation.

Spelling	Many Indian names lend themselves to different spellings. The 'i' in a name is often replaced by 'ee'. For example, the name Nita can also be written as Neeta.
Uniqueness	Most parents today wish to give their child a unique name, a name which is very different. A child with an uncommon name feels good that he/she has a unique name. Many parents also combine names to give an unusual name to their child.
Initials	Before the parents finally settle for a name, they should also consider the child's initials. It can be embarrassing to have an initial like DAD or DUD.
	So when naming your child, check out the initials that he/she will have as a result.

BIRTHSTONES AND FLOWERS

January
Birthstone   :   garnet
Flower   :   carnation

February
Birthstone   :   amethyst
Flower   :   violet

March
Birthstone   :   aquamarine
Flower   :   jonquil

April
Birthstone   :   diamond
Flower   :   sweet pea

May
Birthstone   :   emerald
Flower   :   lily of the valley

June
Birthstone   :   pearl
Flower   :   rose

July
Birthstone	:	ruby
Flower	:	lackspur

August
Birthstone	:	peridot
Flower	:	gladioli

September
Birthstone	:	sapphire
Flower	:	aster

October
Birthstone	:	opal
Flower	:	calendula

November
Birthstone	:	topaz
Flower	:	chrysanthemum

December
Birthstone	:	turquoise
Flower	:	narcissus

Aabharikaa: one who has a halo around her head

Aabhirika: a cowherd's wife

Aadhya: one of the ten forms of Durga

Aaditi: the earth

Aakranti: night, force

Aakuti: inclination, wish

Aalapini: a singer

Aanadparna: one who has wings of joy

Abha: splendour; light; colour; mien, reflection; beauty; resemblance; glory
Abhati, Abhikhya

Abhati: splendour; light

Abheri: fearless; a *ragini*

Abhidha: name

Abhigya: expert; intelligent

Abhikhya: radiant; fame

Abhilasha: longing, wish; affection
Abhilashin

Abhilashin: one who wishes for

Abhivibha: enlightening

Abigail: one of the wives of King David; father's joy

Adhya: one of the ten Durgas; beyond understanding; the first creator

Adilakshmi: Lakshmi

Adishakti: Parvati; the original energy

Adrija: daughter of the mountains; goddess Parvati
Adrika

10

Adrika: a small mountain; name of an *apsara*

Adrika: small mountain

Adya: Durga; unmatched; first; the earth

Afifah: another name for Hazrat Fatimah Zahra; honest; pure; humble

Agaja: Parvati; produced on a mountain

Ahana: immortal, one who cannot be killed; a person who is born during the day

Ahwana: bidding, call

Ahwanita: desired; invited; guest

Aishah: wife of Prophet Muhammad; flourishing; lucky; joyous

Aishah: wife of Prophet Muhammad; lucky; flourishing

Aishwarya: prosperity

Ajira: Durga; swift; quick; a river

Akhilaa: complete whole

Aksayini: not dying

Akshiti: not perishable

Alaknanda: a young girl, one of the names of river Ganga

Alihat: idol; goddess

Alopa: one who has no wishes or desires

Amala: Lakshmi; blemish-free; pure; shining

Amaraja: daughter of the gods

Ambala: mother; affectionate; loving; tender Ambali, Ambalika, Ambi, Ambika

Ambali: mother; affectionate; tender; loving

Ambalika: mother; affectionate; tender; loving

Ambhini: born of water

Ambi: mother; affectionate; tender; loving

Ambika: Parvati; mother; affectionate; loving; good woman

Aminya: pure; clean; untouched

Amirah: full; rich; grand; ruler; princess

Amisha: honest

Amiti: without limits

Amiya: nectar; compassionate; gentle

Amodini: aromatic; illustrious
Amohanika

Amogha: Durga; productive; victorious

Amohanika: aromatic

Amrisha: real

Amshula: bright; radiant

Anabhra: cloudless; clarity of thought

Anadhika: without a superior

Anadya: without a beginning; immortal;
divine; name of an apsara

Anagha: sinless, innocent; clean; perfect

Anala: made of fire; without any blemish;
one of the daughters of Daksh; wife of
Kashyap; mother of trees and creepers

Analupriya: beloved of fire; wife of Agni

Anamika: without a name; the ring finger

Anamra: twisted, favourable

Anandi: Gauri; bestower of pleasure

Anati: humble, full of respect; bent

Ananta: without an end, immortal; divine; the earth; another name for Parvati

Anantika: simple

Anantya: small

Ananya: unequalled

Anasuya: without hatred; one of the daughters of Kardama and Devahuti; wife of sage Atri

Anata: straight; a daughter of Atri and Anasuya; the mother of fruits

Anavi: humane, kind to people

Anindya: beyond condemnation

Anita: guileless

Anitya: momentary

Anjali: homage

Anjasi: honest, deceitless

Ankushi: one of the 24 Jain goddesses

Annada: Durga

Anniksha: to look, gaze

Annishvari: Bhairavi, a fearsome form of
Durga

Anshumala: a garland of rays; a halo

Ansruta: not heard of; unique

Antika: elder sister

Anubha: lightning

Anubhavya: learnt through experience;
divine truth

Anubhuti: experience

Anula: tamed; gentle; agreeable; a female
Arhat or Buddhist saint

Anuli: homage

Anumati: full of love

Anunita: prayer; affability

Anupa: a pond

Anupa: without an equal; unique; a pond;
bank of a river; a sage

Anupriya: incomparable

Anuradha: one who is pleased to worship

Anurima: fond; attached

Anusheela: a devoted servant

Anuttama: best among all

Anvita: one who bridges the gap

Anya: boundless

Aparajita: a form of Durga worshipped on Dussehra; one who is unconquered

Aparna: a name for Parvati who gave up eating everything including leaves so as to win Shiva as her husband; without leaves

Araman: the Vedic goddess of piety

Aranyani: wilderness; desert; forest; the goddess of wilderness

Aravinda: lotus

Archisha: the Vedic goddess of vegetation; flame

Arhana: worship; honoured; adored

Arikta: full; ample; contented

Aripra: blemish-free, clear; virtuous; honest

Arishta: Durga; guarded; undamaged; unharmed

Arja: dustless; pious; clear

Arjika: one who pleads for mercy

Arkasuta: daughter of the sun; another name for Yamuna

Arohi: rising, growing

Arpita: one who is given away

Artika: elder sister

Arundhati: loyalty

Aruni: gold; ruby; glowing red; red cow; dawn; treasured; enlightening; ardent; sacred; Aruna as a female in Indra's assembly

Aryaki: Durga; respected; honoured

Ashivuka: little mare

Ashnaa: daughter of King Bali

Ashni: flash of lightning

Asikni: a holy river

Atiriya: beloved; adored; pursued; rare

Atmaja: Parvati; born of the soul

Avara: Parvati; youngest; inferior

Avisya: desire; warmth

Ayati: a descendant; grandeur; heirs

Azizah: beloved; rare, precious

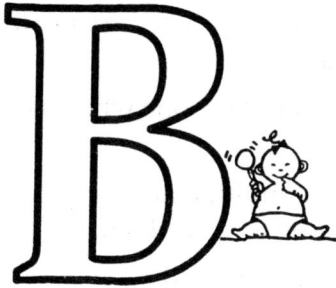

Babhrani: Durga; covered in fire; wandering; present everywhere; descendant of sage Babhru

Bachendri: the sense of speech; tongue

Badarayani: novel; young; clean; perfume

Badari: the Jujube tree

Bagesri: prosperity

Bahair: beautiful, delicate woman

Bahar: spring; orange; rose; glory; elegance, beauty

Bahula: wide; plenty; a cow; indigo; cardamoms
Bahuli, Bahulika

Bahuli: numerous; multiplied; one who has many facets

Bahulika: many times; multiplied; multifaceted personality; the Pleiades

Bahulika: numerous, augmented

Bakula: the flower of the bakula tree; looking like a crane; enduring; vigilant; alert
Bakuli, Bakulita, Bakulika

Bakuli: lady of the blossoms; nature

Bakulika: a flower of the bakula tree

Bakulita: adorned with bakula blossoms

Balada: giver of strength; a daughter of Raudrasva

Balaja: born of power; a beautiful woman; the earth

Balanikarnika: Durga; one possessed with rays of power

Balapushpita: young blossom; strong scented Jasmine

Balini: mighty, strong; the constellation of *Asvini*

Banasuta: daughter of Bana

Bandhini: one who binds; imprisoned

Bandhura: wavy; pretty; charming

Barhayita: as beautiful as the eye on a
peacock feather
Barhidhvaja, Barhina

Barhidhvaja: symbolised by a peacock;
surrounded by a peacock

Barhina: decorated with peacock feathers

Bathsheba: a wife of King David; daughter of
the oath

Bela: wave

Benazir: unequalled; matchless; without
comparison; peerless

Beniyaz: without any wants; without any
worries; another name for God

Bethany: a village near Jerusalem where
Lazarus lived; house of figs

Beulah: a name for Israel; land of Beulah; married

Bhadra: a form of Durga; pretty; good; lucky; flourishing; mild; joyous

Bhadrika: name of the source of the river Ganga

Bhagvati: Lakshmi; a goddess who is an amalgamation of universal self and nature

Bhagya: fate, destiny; fortune, luck; happiness **Bhagyalakshmi, Bhagyasri**

Bhagyalakshmi: goddess of fortune; a name for Lakshmi

Bhaima: descendent of Bhima

Bhairavi: dreadful; consort of Bhairav; a terrifying form of Kali, a *raag*; one of the forms of Durga

Bhakti: devotion

Bhama: shining; animated; gracious; good-looking illustrious; affectionate

Bhamika: gay; productive; flourishing; with a taste for beautiful

Bhamini: shining, radiant; beautiful; glorious; the wife of King Aviksit of Vaishali

Bhanavi: descendant of the sun, as brilliant as the sun; sacred; shining; a river crossed by Rama and Lakshman; another name for the Yamuna river

Bhanuja: daughter of the sun; another name for the Yamuna river

Bhanyatta: one with a regal splendour

Bhargavi: Lakshmi; Parvati; glowing; beautiful; pretty

Bhattarika: Durga; virtuous woman; pious; worshipped

Bhavaja: born of the heart; pretty; honest affectionate

Bhavana: faith; desire

Bhavanika: resident of a castle

Bhavika: natural

Bhaviki: real; pure; natural; compassionate

Bhavila: worthy; good

Bhavini: encouraging; emotions; virtuous; pretty; famous; affectionate; sensitive

Bhavinia: one who induces emotion; noble; pretty; famous; affectionate

Bhavitra: the nature as a form of the earth

Bhavma: belonging to the earth; firm; fixed

Bhavyaa: magnificent; good; calm; worthy; another name for Parvati

Bhavyakirti: famous; intelligent

Bhimasika: enemy of the terrible; mighty, strong; without any fear

Bhomira: born of the earth; the coral; productive; patient

Bhraji: shine; glory, fame

Bhramee: full of shine

Bhumayi: full of existence; born from the earth

Bhumi: earth, soil; an object of existence; the earth as a goddess who was the daughter of Brahma and wife of Mahavishnu

Bhumija: born of the earth; a name for Sita

Bhuva: fire; the earth

Bhuvaneshwarya: Lakshmi; it is believed that the goddess holds a pitcher of nectar in one hand and a bell in another which is constantly ringing to proclaim her victory; she is always victorious

Binita: modest

Brahmani: consort of Brahma; river; a name for Durga

Brahmani: Sarasvati; the consort of Brahma

Brihanta: destroyer of the powerful; mighty; great

Carmela: Mount Carmel in Israel is believed to be a paradise; garden; vineyard

Chaitali: intelligent; belonging to the mind

Chaitri: born during the spring time; as beautiful and soft and fresh as a new blossom; always happy

Chakrika: a name for Lakshmi

Chaksani: pleasing to the eyes; illuminating

Chakshushi: observer; seer

Chalama: ever moving goddess; a name for Parvati

Chana: love: wish

Chanchala: changeable; always moving; lightning; a river; another name for Lakshmi

Chandalika: belonging to a low caste; a name for Durga

Chandashri: celestial moon; fair; good-looking; peaceful; gracious

Chandavata: impetuous; fiery; one of the eight forms of Durga

Chandnika: a small sandalwood tree

Chandrabala: daughter of the moon; a girl as beautiful as the moon

Chandrakanta: as lovely as the moon; dear to the moon; moonlight
Chandrakanti

Chandrakanti: as shining as the moon; silver; moonlight

Chandrakriti: shaped as a moon; as beautiful as the moon

Chandralara: the moon and the stars together

Chandralekha: a digit of the moon

Chandrama: moonlight

Chandrarupa: Lakshmi; with a moon-like face

Chandrasahodari: Lakshmi; as radiant as the moon; it is believed that Lakshmi is the moon's sister because both came forth from the Ocean of Milk when it was churned by gods

Chandrashila: moonstone; calm; composed; tranquil; pleasing

Chandri: moonlight; fair; cool; soothing

Chandrika: moonlight; fair; calm; cool; soothing; fenugreek; cardamom

Chandrima: moonlight

Chantni: beloved

Chapala: unsteady; efficient; lightning; a name for Lakshmi

Charchika: Durga; aromatic; repetition of a word

Chardrali: moonbeam

Charnapuraa: full moon; fair; beautiful; soothing; tranquil

Charshani: quick; efficient; moonlight; saffron

Charuangi: one with a beautiful body

Charubala: a beautiful girl

Charudhi: one who has an auspicous mind

Charulata: a beautiful creeper

Charushila: a beautiful jewel

Charuvi: grand; another name for Kubera's wife, Bhadra

Charvangi: one with a beautiful body

Chaturika: clever; skilful

Chavi: an image; reflection; beauty; grandeur; a ray of light

Chaya: a form of Durga known as Katyayani; shade; hue; pretty; shine; shadow

Cheshta: effort; movement

Chetaki: capable of perceiving or feeling things; Spanish jasmine; black myrobalan

Chetna: wisdom; mind; knowledge; comprehension

Chitra: picture; beautiful; anything that attracts the eye

Chitrai: the spring; the month of April

Chitralata: a beautiful creeper

Chitralekha: beautiful outline; portrait

Chitrali: a wonderful lady; a friend

Chitrangi: one with a beautiful body

Chitrani: another name for river Ganga

Chitrarathi: one with a bright chariot; a form of Durga

Chitrarati: bestower of excellent gifts

Chitrashri: one bestowed with divine beauty

Chitrini: one who possesses various talents; brightly ornamented; possesses marks of excellence

Chitrita: adorned with ornaments; painted

Comsuelo: Saint Mary of consolation is a name for Virgin Mary; consolation

D

Dadhija: Lakshmi; who is believed to be the daughter of the ocean and emerged from the Ocean of Milk; daughter of milk; born of curd

Dakshaya: one who strives for perfection; perfect

Dakshayani: coming from Daksha; gold or an ornament made of gold; daughter of a perfect being; daughter of Daksha; another name for goddess Durga

Dakshayaninya: obtained from Daksha; gold; golden; ornament; daughter of a perfect being

Dakshina: donation to an officiating priest or to god; apt; righthanded

Damani: lightning

Damayanti: one who subdues men; self-restrained

Darnika: sacrificial ladle or spoon

Darpana: looking glass

Darpanika: a small looking glass

Darpita: proud

Darshani: Durga; beautiful; pretty; worth looking at

Darshita: exhibited; displayed

Darshtashri: one with noticeable beauty

Dashmee: the tenth day of the lunar fortnight

Daya: pity; mercy

Dayadi: one who inherits; daughter; heiress

Dayita: compassionate; beloved; cherished; dear

Deetya: Lakshmi; one who answers all prayers of the devotees

Dehini: the earth

Delilah: the companion of Samson; thinker

Deshna: gift; offering

Deshtri: pointer; indicator

Deti: radiance; glowing; beauty

Devahuti: invocation of gods

Devajaya: wife of a god

Devala: attached to the gods; music personified

Devalekha: a divine line; with a divine outline; a celestial beauty

Devanani: one with a divine voice

Devaniti: enjoyment of the gods; pleasing to gods

Devashri: Lakshmi; divine; goddess

Devayani: chariot of the gods; invested with divine power

Deveshi: chief of the goddess; a name for Durga

Devesmita: with a divine smile; heroine of *Katha Saritsagara*

Devika: minor goddess; god-like; a class of goddess of an inferior order

Deviki: derived from a goddess

Devina: resembling a goddess

Devishi: Durga; chief of the goddesses

Devkulya: divine pitcher; belonging to the gods; a name for holy Ganga

Devsmita: one with a divine smile

Dhamini: religious, pious; a type of perfume

Dhanishta: residing in wealth; very wealthy

Dhanvanya: treasure of the jungle; an oasis

Dhanya: virtuous; good; granter of wealth

Dhara: the earth

Dharini: possessing something; a mystical verse to be used; assuage pain; a daughter of Svadha; the wife of

Agnimitra; the earth personified as wife of Dhruva

Dharitree: the earth

Dhatreyika: supporter; nurse; confidante; a maid of Draupad

Dhenuka: a milch cow; a celestial river

Dhisha: direction; path

Dhishana: knowledge; wisdom; grace; goddesses, the goddess of abundance; the wife of Havirdhana, daughter of Agni

Dhishana: wisdom; intelligence; speech; praise; hymn; goddess

Dhita: born of a bird; a daughter

Dhiti: thought; wisdom; reflection; prayer

Dhriti: fixed; order; constant; happiness personified as the daughter of Daksha; wife of Dharma; a goddess; one of the sixteen digits of the moon; the wife of Rudra Manu

Dhruti: Durga; courageous

Dhulika: pollen of flowers

Dhumini: hazy, smoky

Dhumra: Durga; hazy

Dhyeya: ideal; aim

Didhi: resolve; shining; firmness
    Didhiti

Didhiti: fixed, stable; devotion; inspiration

Diksha: initiation into a religious order; the
    initiation personified as the wife of Soma,
    Rudra, Ugra and Rudra Vamadeva

Dinah : a daughter of Jacob and Leah;
    avenging

Dipakalika: flame of a lamp

Dipaksi: bright-eyed

Dipali: rows of lights

Dipana: bright; passion; that which kindles
    in flames; an attendant of Devi

Dipanjali: a lamp for praying

Dipra: shining; bright

Dirghika: a tall girl; an oblong lake; a daughter of Visvakarman

Dishti: good fortune

Divija: born of the sky; born of heaven; divine, a god

Divolka: fallen from the sky; a meteor

Divya: radiance

Dolores: Saint Mary of the Sorrows — is a name for the Virgin Mary; sorrowful

Dridha: firm, fixed; fortress

Drshika: pretty, beautiful

Druhi: daughter

Druti: softened; the wife of Naksa and mother of Gaya

Dyotana: shining; bright

Dyukhsa: heavenly

Dyuthi: shining; bright

Eden: the paradise on earth; happiness

Eka: Durga; solitary; unique; unequalled

Ekacharini: woman devoted to a single man, obedient; loyal; virtuous woman

Ekaja: only child

Ekakini: solitary; alone

Ekamati: concentrated

Ekanansa: Durga, Subhadra; the wife of Arjuna and the sister of Krishna; new moon

Ekangika: made of sandalwood; fair; often; auspicious; loved by the gods

Ekanta: beautiful

Ekantika: devoted to one objective

Ekaparna: single-leafed; living on a single leaf; the daughter of Himavana and Mena; the sister of Durga, Aparna and Ekapatala and the wife of sage Devata

Ekastaka: a collection of eight

Ekavali: a string of pearls

Ekisha: a goddess; the foremost goddess

Eksika: eye

Ekta: unity

Ela: the earth

Eleora: the lord is my light

Eliana: a feminine form of Elisha

Elizabeth: the mother of John the Baptist; dedicated to God

Elokshi: one who has thick hair

Emmanulle: a feminine form of Emmanuel; God is with everybody

Ena: doe; spotted; a black antelope; another name for the zodiac sign of Capricorn

Enaksi: doe-eyed

Eni: deer; flowing stream

Esha: objective; wish, desire

Eshanika: fulfilling wishes; a goldsmith's balance

Eshita: wanted; longing

Esikha: one who has achieved the objective; an arrow; a dart

Etaha: shining

Eti: arrival

Eunice: mother of Saint Timothy; joyous; triumphant

Eve: the first woman created by God

Faghar: flower

Faghiyat: henna blossom

Faham: understanding; wise

Fahamat: understanding

Fahimati: wise; prudent

Fahwat: good quality honey

Faiha: expanse; fragrant, aromatic

Faihah: perfume, fragrance

Fainan: one with beautiful, luscious hair

Faiqah: superior

Faizah: beneficient

Fakahat: one with a good nature

Fakirah: excellent; precious

Fana: wealth; perfume

Fanhanah: a female artist

Fannan: an artist

Faqa: deepred colour

Faqihah: a woman well-versed in law and
divinity; theologian; school mistress

Farah: joy, happiness, gay

Faranah: one who is famous; glorious;
Faridun's mother

Farhanah: glad; joyful

Faridah: solitary; different; large pearl

Farihah: a good-natured woman

Farihah: happy woman

Farya: friend

Farzi: queen at chess

Farzin: intelligent; wise; queen at chess

Fasah: break forth and shine in full splendour

Fasanah: a tale, fable; famous

Fasha: one who speaks well

Fatat: a young girl

Fatimah: daughter of Prophet Muhammad

Fazanah: intelligent

Firzan: queen in chess

Fisa: peacock

Frashmi: prosperity; giving; an epithet of Haoma

Frayashti: worship; praise

Freya: dear

Freyana: dear

Frohar: an angel; a sublime spirit which protects the soul as a guardian angel

G

Gabrielle: a feminine form of Gabriel; dedicated to God

Gajagamini: with gait as graceful as an elephant **Gajagati**

Gajagati: with gait as graceful as an elephant

Gamati: with a flexible mind

Gambhari: one who reaches the sky

Gambhirika: deep; river

Gananayika: consort of the lord of ganu's; another name for goddess Parvati and Ganeshani

Gandha: aromatic; a name for goddess Parvati

Gandhali: aromatic

Gandhalika: aromatic; an apsara; another name for goddess Parvati and Satyavati; the mother of Vyasa
Gandhali, Gandharika

Gandhamohini: one with an enchanting fragrance

Gandhari: belonging to Gandhar

Gandharika: the process of preparing perfume

Gandharvi: the speech of a gandharv; the granddaughter of sage Kashyap and Krodhvasha; the daughter of Surabhi and the mother of horses; another name for Durga; a seductive water nymph who haunts the banks of rivers

Gandhini: aromatic; another name for Prithvi

Ganeshagit: song of Ganesha

Ganeshani: consort of Ganesha

Gangi: Durga; Ganga-like; as holy as the river Ganga

Gangika: like the river Ganga; one who is as holy, pure as the river Ganga

Gangotri: the source of the river Ganga; a pilgrimage spot

Ganika: female elephant

Ganikarika: made from grass

Ganita: dexterous; full of good qualities

Ganjan: surpassing; excelling

Ganya: garden of the lord

Gargi: churn; a learned woman born in the Garga family

Garima: grace; divinity; grandeur

Garvari: Durga; arrogant

Gathika: a song

Gati: comprehension skills; speed; guit

Gaunika: valuable; the jasmine flower

Gaurangi: fair, cow-coloured

Gauri: Parvati; fair; cow-coloured; yellow; pretty

Gaurika: like Gauri, fair, pretty

Gautami: one who destroys darkness; a name for rivers Godavari, Gomti; goddess Durga

Gayanti: belonging to Gaya; wife of king Gaya, the royal sage

Gayantika: singing; a Himalayan cave

Gayatri: 3 phased verse; a vedic *mantra*; a name for Sarasvati

Gayatrini: one who sings hymns of the *Sama Veda*

Geshna: a singer

Ghazal: a lyric poem; words of love sonnet; love poetry

Ghritachi: full of water

Ghughari: bracdet of jingling bells

Ghurnika: one who whirls

Gira: Sarasvati; a vedic hymn; a song; word, speech; language

Giribala: daughter of the mountain; a name for Parvati
Giribhu, Girija, Girijamba, Giriganga

Giribhu: coming from the mountains; as name for Ganga and Parvati

Girija: daughter of the mountain; a name for Parvati

Girijamba: daughter of the mountain; a name for Parvati

Girika: the peak of a mountain; the daughter of river Saktimati

Girikarni: a lotus

Girisha: Parvati; lady of the mountains

Girishma: summer

Girisuta: Parvati; daughter of the mountain

Girni: praise; famous person

Gita: song, lyric, poem; a religious book of the Hindus consisting of sermon given by Lord Krishna to Arjuna during the battle of Mahabharata

Gitali: lover of song

Gitanjali: devotional singing of a hymn

Gitashri: the divine *Gita*

Giti: song

Gopika: one who looks after the herd; another name for Radha

Gorma: Parvati; worthy of considering

Gramani: ladies of the village

Gulfroz: as beautiful as a flower

Gulika: ball; anything round

Gulmini: a group; creeper

Guneha: flower; bird

Gunita: talented; virtuous

Gunja: humming; a cluster of blossoms

Gunjika: humming; images; meditation; the rosary pea

Gurnika: wife of a teacher; a companion of Devayani

Gutika: small ball; a pearl; a cocoon of silkworm

Habibah: another name for the city of Medina; beloved; sweetheart

Hafsah: wife of Prophet Muhammad; to collect; to rest; lion's cub

Hagar: Sarah's handmaiden; the mother of Ishmael; abandoned; unknown

Haima: of the snow; golden; another name for Parvati and Ganga

Halah: sister of Prophet Muhammad; the halo that surrounds the moon or sun; fame

Halipriya: beloved of Vishnu, the Kadamba tree

Hamra: the colour red; fair woman

Hannah: the mother of Samuel; affable

Hansanadini: talking like a swan, a woman with a thin waist, a gait as graceful as an elephant and the voice of a cuckoo Hansanandini, Hansapada, Hansini, Hansaveni, Hansika, Hansi

Hansanandini: daughter of a swan

Hansapada: the foot of the swan

Hansaveni: Sarasvati; with plait like a swan; with a good plait

Hansi: swan; goose

Hansika: swan; a daughter of Surabhi who is said to support the southern region

Hansini: swan; goose

Hanum: a lady, woman

Harasnti: one that delights

Harbala: daughter of Shiva

Hardika: affectionate

Hardika: sincere

Haridra: turmeric

Harikanta: Lakshmi; dear of Vishnu

Harikina: completely concentrated on Vishnu

Harinaksi: doe-eyed

Harini: doe; greenery; yellow jasmine; a golden image; an apsara

Haritalika: bringer of greenery; goddess of fertility; fourth day of the bright half of the month of *Bhadra* personified as a goddess of pleasure

Hariti: yellowish-brown colour; green; fresh; the goddess of Rajgriha

Harmya: house; palace; mansion

Harshala: happy

Harshini: pleasnt, happy

Harshita: full of happiness

Harshvina: a lute that delights

Hasika: blooming; smiling; spreading happiness

Hasnat: beautiful; fair

Hastha: a star

Hasumati: one who laughs always

Hataki: a river formed by bringing together Shiva and Parvati

Hayi: wish, desire

Hela: moonlight; easily done

Hema: golden; the earth; good-looking

Hemabha: appearing like gold

Helika: sister of Hiranyakshipur; lighting of ceremonial fire

Hemakshi: golden-eyed

Hemalata: golden vine

Hemamala: golden garland

Hemanarna: golden-complexioned

Hemangi: girl with a golden body

Hemangini: girl with a golden body

Hemani: Parvati; as valuable as gold; made of gold

Hemanti: belonging to winter

Hemaprabha: golden light

Hemapuspika: with small golden flowers

Hemaragini: coloured with gold

Hemavarna: golden-complexioned

Hemayathika: woven with gold; the yellow Jasmine

Himaja: daughter of the snow; daughter of the Himavana; another name for Parvati

Himalini: completely covered with snow

Himani: glacier; snow; avalanche; another name for Parvati

Himasuta: Parvati; daughter of the snow; fair-complexioned; tranquil; reposed

Hina: aroma

Hiranya: golden

Hityshi: well-wisher

Hityshini: well-wisher

Hiya: heart

Hrada: lake, pond

Hrdayagandha: fragrance of the heart

I

Iaikhyata: unity

Iaiktya: unity

Iaishwarya: wealth

Ian: God is benevolent

Ibha: elephant; the number eight

Ibhi: female elephant

Ida: a moment; wisdom; the earth as a giver of food; the daughter of Vayu, who was the wife of Dhruv and mother of Utkal

Idika: belonging to Ida; another name for Prithvi or the earth

Iditri: one who appreciates

Iha: longing, wish

Ihita: wished for

Ijya: an image; a gift; charity; worship

Ikia: in God lies my salvation

Iksha: sight

Ikshenya: worth-looking

Ikshita: visible, seen

Ikshulata: creeper of sweetness

Ikshumalini: one who is sweet

Ikshuvari: sugarcane juice

Ikslada: that which renders sweetness; sweet-tongued

Ila: Durga; earth; oblation, appreciation; prayer; mother; teacher; priestess

Ilabila: one who is appreciated; protector of the earth

Ilakshi: eye of the earth; the axis of the earth; centre of the earth

Ilanila: one who possesses insight; scholar; appreciation

Ilesha: queen of the earth

Ilhana: music; sweet voice

Ilika: belonging to the earth; momentary; small; earth, a minor form of the earth

Ilina: very intelligent

Ilniak: protector of the earth

Ilrika: protector of the earth; the five stars at the head of the constellation Orion

Impana: sweet-voiced

Inakshi: sharp-eyed

Indabala: daughter of Indra

Indata: the power and dignity of Indra

Indira: Lakshmi; granter of prosperity

Indivarini: a cluster of blue lotuses

Indrabha: light of Indra

Indrakshi: one who has eyes like Indra; a
goddess

Indramohini: one to whom Indra is attracted

Indrani: consort of Indra

Indranilika: as blue as Indra

Indrayani: wife of Indra

Indu: a bright drop

Indubhava: coming from the moon

Induja: daughter of the moon; a name for the
river Narmada

Indulekha: a digit of the moon

Inika: small earth

Ipsa: longing, wish

Ipsita: wished for, longed for

Ira: Sarasvati; the earth; water; nourishment;
speech

Iraja: daughter of the wind

Irama: happiness of the earth

Iravati: full of water or milk; clouds

Irijaya: victorious; wind

Isha: Durga; the pole of a plough

Ishaana: Durga; chief

Ishani: ruling; the wood from sami tree
which when rubbed produces fire;
another name for Durga

Ishanika: belonging to the north-east

Ishi: Durga; a goddess

Ishika: a painter's brush; the pen used for
writing auspicious things

Ishita: wished for

Ishta: that which is worshipped through
sacrifice; the sami tree

Ishtara: dearer

Ishtu: desire, wished for

Ishuka: arrow like; an arrow

Ishvari: a name for Parvati, best among the
  divine

itara: another

Itkila: aromatic, full of fragrance

Ivria: belonging to the land of Abraham

Iya: present everywhere

Jagavi: born of the world

Jagriti: awakening; rising

Jagti: belonging to the universe; heaven and
hell together; another name for the earth

Jahnavi: born from the ear; the daughter of
Jahnu; another name for the river Ganga

Jaijaivanti: the song of victory, full of victory

Jaimala: garland of victory

Jaiprabha the light of victory

Jaipriya: beloved of victory

Jaishila: one who is always victorious

Jaisudha: nectar of victory

Jaitvati: bearer of victory

Jaivahini: victorious army

Jalabala: Lakshmi; one who lives in water; daughter of the water

Jaladhij: Lakshmi; daughter of the ocean

Jaladhija: daughter of the ocean; a name for Lakshmi

Jalaja: Lakshmi; born of the water; the lotus flower

Jalajakshi: lotus-eyed

Jalajini: cluster of lotuses

Jalakusuma: flower in the water

Jalambika: mother of water

Jalapriya: dear to water

Jalaprya: beloved of water

Jalavalika: surrounded by water; lightning

Jalbala: maiden of water; daughter of water

Jalela: goddess of water

Jallata: a stream of water; a wave

Jama: daughter

Janaki: Sita, daughter of king Janak

Jane: a feminine form of John; God is gracious

Janestha: wanted by men; the Spanish jasmine

Janguli: Durga; one who has knowledge of poisons

Janhita: one who thinks about the welfare of mankind

Janice: God is benevolent

Januja: born; a daughter

Jarayer: reproductive

Jarita: old; rotten; a sarngika bird who had four sons by sage Mandapala

Jarul: queen of flowers

Javitri: spice; mace

Javlitri: bright; resplendent; shining

Jaya: victory; victorious

Jayalata: Lakshmi; as good as victory; the
goddess of victory

Jayana: giver of victory; armour; a daughter
of Indra

Jayani: one who brings victory; a daughter of
Indra

Jayanti: one who is victorious in the end; a
flag; a daughter of Indra and the wife of
Sukra

Jayita: victorious

Jayitri: victorious

Jayshri: goddess of victory

Jesusa: in God lies my redemption

Jhala: extreme heat; a girl

Jhankarini: that which produces a tinkling
sound, bell; a woman wearing anklets; a
name for Durga

Jharna: spring; stream; flowing down

Jhatalika: light; shine; splendour

Jhati: shining; glittering

Jhillika: light; moth; sunshine

Jhilmil: shining

Jhilmit: partially visible

Jhumari: ornament of the forehead

Jigisha: one who desires to be victorious

Jitavari: best among victorious

Jitya: victorious

Jivantika: giver of long life

Jivika: the source of life, water; occupation

Joan: God is benevolent

Joelle: a feminine; form of Joel; God is willing

Jonatha: gift of god; a feminine form of
     Jonathan

Joshika: cluster of birds; a young woman

Joshya: happy

Jualitri: lighted, shining flaming

Jugisha: one who wishes to be victorious

Juhi: jasmine flower

Jurni: firebrand; fire burning

Jutika: a type of camphor

Jvalita: burning; bright

Jyesthila: elder; superior

Jyori: flame

Jyotika: with a flame

Jyotiranika: one with a glowing face

Jyotsna: moonlight

Jyotsni: a moonlit night

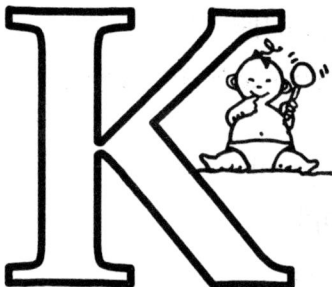

Kaalaka: Durga; pupil of the eye; a female crow; blue; black aromatic earth

Kaalanjari: Parvati; one who resides in the Kalanjara mountain

Kaamakya: Durga; granter of wishes

Kaberi: full of water; a river in south India

Kadali: the banana tree

Kadamba: a cluster; cloud; the kadamba tree
Kadambaki, Kadambari
Kadambaki: blossoms of the kadamba tree

Kadambari: belonging to the kadamba tree; female cuckoo; wine obtained from the kadamba tree; another name for Sarasvati

Kadambini: a garland of clouds

Kahala: impish, naughty; a young woman; a kind of musical instrument; an apsara; Varuna's wife
Kahini

Kahini: impish; naughty; young

Kaikashi: plants that grow in water

Kairanini: born of water

Kairavi: moonlight

Kajal: kohl

Kajri: kohl-coloured, cloud-like, a folksong of Uttar Pradesh sung during the monsoons

Kakali: voice of the cuckoo; a musical instrument

Kakalika: with a low and sweet voice; an apsara

Kakasya: cow-faced; a Buddhist goddess

Kakshi: belonging to the jungle; perfume

Kakubha: summit; peak; quarter of the heavens; splendour; beauty

Kalakarni: Lakshmi; with black ears

Kalandika: one who grants art or skills; wisdom

Kalanjari: residing in the Kalanjara mountain; a name for Parvati

Kalavinka: a sparrow; the Indian cuckoo

Kalchika: black sandalwood

Kalika: Durga; dark blue; black; a flaw in gold

Kalikantha: with a pleasing voice; done; the Indian cuckoo

Kalindi: the river Yamuna which begins its journey from Mount Kalinda

Kalli: ornament of the wrist

Kalloni: one who remains happy always; a fast flowing river or stream

Kalmeshika: spotted

Kalpana: imagination; idea; composition

Kalpani: as blue as the peacock's tail; night-
time

Kalya: apt; pleasant; auspicious

Kalyani: beneficial; auspicious; favourable

Kamakshi: Durga; with beautiful eyes

Kamalakshi: with eyes like a lotus
Kamalika, Kamalini
Kamali: full of desire

Kamalika: a small lotus

Kamalini: lotus plant; a cluster of lotus
blossoms; pretty; aromatic; lucky; dear to
gods

Kamana: desire

Kamayaka: desired abode; the forest in
which the Pandavas hid during their
exile

Kamayani: the mirror of love

Kameshvari: Parvati; the consort of Kameshvar, the lord of desires

Kamini: desirable; beautiful

Kamita: longed for, wished for

Kamra: longed for; pretty; affectionate Kamya

Kamuka: longed for; the Madhavi creeper

Kamuna: wished for

Kamya: pretty; desirable; hard-working; a celestial woman

Kana: girl; an eye

Kanaka: born of sand; another name for Sita

Kanakaa: Sita; born of sand

Kanam: the black soiled earth

Kanavi: small kite

Kanchi: glittering; a waistband with bells; a pilgrimage centre in south India

Kandhara: water bearer; a cloud

Kandire: root-like

Kanika: an atom; very small

Kanina: young; the pupil of the eye

Kanistha: the youngest

Kanita: iris of the eye

Kanka: scent of the lotus; a daughter of
Ugrasena and sister of Kanka

Kankalini: Durga; one with a necklace of
bones

Kankana: a bracelet; an ornament

Kanksha: desire, wish; inclination

Kankshini: one who wishes

Kannaki: Sita; devoted and virtuous wife

Kanta: beloved; a perfume; the earth

Kanti: fame; glory; beauty; a name for
Lakshmi

Kanupriya: Krishna's beloved

Kanyaka: Durga; the youngest; girl; maiden;
daughter; the virgin goddess

Kanyala: girl

Kanyana: girl

Kapalini: consort of Kapali or Shiva; a name for Durga

Kapili: with yellowish-brown coloured waves; a river in Assam

Karala: Durga; opening wide; tearing

Karali: the terrible; Durga in her destructive form

Karalika: Durga; that which tears

Karika: a collection of verses on philosophy

Karkari: a lute

Karmishta: extremely hard-working

Karni: with ears; a good listener

Karnika: creeper; heart of lotus; earring

Karpani: happiness

Karshana: that which belongs to Krishna

Karttiki: the moon night in the month of *Kartik*; sacred; full; holy

Karuna: affectionate; mercy

Karungya: merciful; affectionate; worth appreciating

Kashvi: shining; beautiful

Kastha: peak; important point; appearance; water, the sun; a daughter of Daksha; the wife of Kashyap

Kasturi: scented with musk

Kasturika: musk

Katyayani: attired in red; another name for Parvati

Kaukulika: belonging to the universe; one who considers the universe as his family

Kaumudi: moonlight personified as the wife of Chandra; rejoicing; full moon day in the month of *Kartik*

Kaushalika: gift; an offering

Kaushiki: Durga; concealed; enveloped with silk

Kautirya: Durga; one who resides in a hut

Kaveri: full of water; a courtesan, turmeric; a river in south India

Kavika: poetess

Kawali: bangle

Kenati: above all; another name for Rati, the wife of Kama

Kesarini: saffron-coloured; a lioness

Keshini: Durga; one with long hair

Ketaki: golden, the flower worn on Shiva's head

Kevali: one who has attained the absolute; a Jain who has achieved complete knowledge

Keyurin: one with an armlet

Khadijah: first wife of Prophet Muhammad and the first woman to accept Islam

Kharika: musk

Khyati: Lakshmi; view; observation; idea; knowledge; illustrious; famous; a hymn of praise

Kiya: the cooing of a bird

Krinjala: brook

Krishanga: svelte, slim; bean-bodied Krishangi

Krishangi: slender
Krithika: covered with stars

Kriti: creation

Kritvi: accomplished; talented

Kritya: action; accomplishment; proper; a female deity; a river

Krityaka: full of achievements

Kshamya: the earth

Kshema: Durga; peaceful; tranquil; safety; security

Kshema: safety; security; welfare; peace; another name for Durga

Kshemya: Durga; goddess of welfare

Kshiti: house; home; earth; soil of the earth

Kshitija: born of the earth; another name for Sita

Kuja: Durga; Sita; the daughter of the earth; the horizon

Kunjika: belonging to the bower

Kurangi: a blemish in the moon; deer

Kusamita: adorned with flowers; made of flowers

Laghuvi: gentle; tender; tiny

Lahari: wave

Lakshaki: made of or dyed with lac; another
name for Sita.

Lakshita: visible, seen; another name for Sita

Lakshmi: goddess of prosperity; auspicious;
lucky; shine; lustre

Lalantika: a long necklace

Lalatika: a piece of jewellery worn on the
forehead

Lalita: a form of Durga; woman; beautiful

81

Lalitaka: favourite daughter; an ancient pilgrimage of Brahma

Lalitangi: one with a beautiful body

Lalitasya: affectionate; charming; elegant

Lambusa: a necklace of seven kings

Lasaki: Sita; made of lac

Lata: vine; a string of pearls; a slender woman; the Madhavi creeper

Latabha: beautiful, good-looking

Latika: an ornament of the forehead; a vermilion dot on the forehead; a string of pearls; a small creeper

Lavali: a vine; custard apple Lavalika

Lavalika: a small vine

Lavalina: concentrated; devoted

Lavana: pretty

Lavangi: belonging to the clove plant; an apsara

Lavanya: pretty, beautiful

Leah: the wife of Jacob; tired

Lepakshi: with painted eyes

Libuja: vine

Line: completely absorbed, engrossed

Lipi: alphabet, manuscript

Lipika: the written word; alphabet; anointing

Lisa: dedicated to God

Lochana: the eye; enlightening

Lohitakshi: red-eyed

Lohitika: the gem ruby

Lohitya: rice; the *Puranic* name for river Brahmaputra

Lokajanani: Lakshmi; mother of the world

Lokaloka: glory of the world; one who enlightens people

Lokamatri: Lakshmi; mother of the world

Lokanya: one who is worthy of heaven

Lolika: light, reddish-brown

Lolita: agitated; fickle-minded

Lumbika: a kind of musical instrument

M

Madanika: excited; the daughter of Menaka

Madayanti: exciting; Arabian jasmine; another name for Durga

Madayantika: exciting; Arabian jasmine

Madhavi: sweet; an intoxicating drink; honey; sacred basil; the daughter of King Yayati; another name for Durga and Subhadra

Madhavika: one who collects honey; a creeper

Madhudhara: stream of honey

Madhuja: made of honey; a honeycomb; the earth

Madhukasha: whip of sweetness; dew

Madhulika: sweetness; a kind of bee

Madhumita: sweet friend

Madhupratika: one with a beautiful mouth

Madhuri: sweetness; appealing wine: a kind musical instrument

Madhurima: sweetness; beautiful

Madhvija: born of honey; an intoxicating drink

Madira: nectar; wine; another name for Durga; another name for the wife of Varuna and the goddess of wine

Madri: the princess of Madra; wife of Krishna

Madura: a bird

Magadhi: belonging to Magadha

Maghi: one who distributes gifts

Maghya: born in the month of *Magha*, the blossom of jasmine

Mahajaya: extremely victorious

Mahajva: very fast; fleet-footed

Mahakshi: belonging to the sky

Mahallika: a female attendant a; daughter of Prahlada

Mahanisha: the greatest of the nights; a name for Durga

Mahasveta: very white; a name for Durga and Sarasvati

Mahelika: a woman

Maheshvari: Durga; great goddess; a river

Mahika: dew; frost

Mahima: grandeur; power

Mahishi: queen; belonging to a high rank

Mahita: flowing on the earth, river; greatness,

Mahiya: joyful; delight

Mahiya: joyous; very happy

Maholka: great meteor

Mahuli: one with a good voice

Maimunah: wife of Prophet Muhammad; lucky; auspicious

Maina: intelligence

Maithili: Sita; belonging to Mithila

Maitrayani: belonging to Mitra; friendly Maitreyi, Maitri

Maitreyi: friendly, affable

Maitri: companionship; generosity; goodwill

Makshika: bee

Malaikah: the 35th *Surah* of the *Quran*; angels

Malashika: garlanded; a *ragini*

Malati: jasmine; bud; flower; maid; virgin Malatika

Malatika: made of jasmine

Malavi: princess of the Malavas; the wife of King Asvapati of Madra; a *ragini*

Malavika: belonging to Malva; the heroine of a drama by Kalidasa

Malini: Durga; aromatic, pleasant smelling; a female gardener

Mallika: jasmine; daughter; necklace; intoxicating drink; queen

Maluka: the sared basil

Manaka: according to the mind; a loving woman a female elephant

Manani: wife of Manu

Mananya: one who is worthy of appreciation

Manapritia: one who is dear to heart; happiness; joy

Manasa: conceived in the mind; mind; heart

Manasvi: one who controls the mind; wise

Manasvini: Durga; one who has mind in control; noble; proud; good

Manavi: wife of Manu; daughter of man

Manavika: a young girl

Manayi: Manu's wife

Mandara: slow; large; fixed; a pearl chain of strings

Mandarika: the Indian Coral tree

Mandavi: an able administrator; the wife of Bharat

Mandavika: related to administration

Mandhari: bearer of honour

Mandira: belonging to a temple; pious; melodious

Mandira: belonging to the temple; pious, holy; a slow sound; metallic cymbals producing a musical sound

Mandra: pleasant; affable; charming; low voiced

Mangala: Durga; auspicious; fortunate; a faithful wife

Manika: jewellery; a particular weight

Manimala: Lakshmi; a necklace of jewels; beautiful

Maninga: treasure of jewels; a river

Manini: determined; self-respecting; an apsara

Manishi: longed by the heart

Manishika: comprehended; wisdom

Manisita: wisdom

Maniya: glass bead

Manja: a cluster of blossoms

Manjari: cluster of blossoms, spring; stalk of a flower

Manjarika: a small cluster of blossoms, a small pearl

Manjulika: good-looking

Manjushri: Lakshmi; ethereal beauty

Manorita: belonging to the mind; longing

Manthini: that which churns

Mantika: contemplative; an *Upanishad*

Mantrana: advice

Mantrini: the queen of chess

Manushi: woman; soft-hearted

Manya: one who deserves respect

Manyanti: respectable

Marali: female swan

Maralika: small swan

Marichika: mirage; illusion

Mariyah: one of the wives of Prophet
    Muhammad; one with a fair complexion

Marshthi: one who lives in cleanliness;
    washing; purification

Martha: a sister of the Virgin Mary; lady;
    unhappy

Mary: mother of Jesus; bitter

Marya: the limit

Marziyah: another name for Hazrat Fatimah Zahra; one who is liked by all

Masumah: title of Hazrat Fatimah Zahra; innocent; guarded

Matali: mother's friend; an attendant of Durga

Matalli: anything excellent

Matallika: anything excellent of its kind

Matri: Durga; Lakshmi; one who has true knowledge

Matrika: divine mother

Mayuranki: with peacock marks; a jewel

Mayurika: with peacock feathers; a *ragini*

Medha: a form of Sarasvati; wise, sagacious

Medhani: wise; the consort of Brahma

Medhya: fresh; clean; holy; wise; intelligent

Medini: the earth; fertile

Mekhala: belt; the slope of a mountain; another name for river Narmada

Menaja: a name for Parvati

Menita: intelligent

Midhushi: abundant

Mihika: mist; fog; snow

Minali: a fisherwoman; another name for Satyavati

Minati: fish-like; voluptuous

Mitali: friendship

Mitusi: one who has limited needs

Mrgisna: doe-eyed

Mridani: Parvati; consort of Mrid

Mridvika: soft; gentle; mild

Mrigekshana: deer-eyed

Mrinali: lotus stalk

Mrinalika: a lotus root

Mrinalini: a lotus; aromatic; holy; dear to gods

Mringangi: soft-bodied; delicate

Mritsa: earth; aromatic soil

Mritsna: earth; very fertile soil

Mrkshini: a rain cloud

Mrtfika: the earth

Mruda: Parvati; affecionate

Muralika: a small flute

N

Naazima: song

Nabhanya: arising from the heaven; heavenly

Nadantika: destroying; a river of ancient India

Nagarini: civic; civilised

Nagija: daughter of the serpent

Naidhrua: Parvati; almost perfect

Naima: trying to be one with the absolute

Nainika: pupil of the eye

Nainika: pupil of the eye

Nakanari: heavenly woman

Nakavanita: heavenly woman

Nakti: night

Nakuli: a wife of Shiva

Nalada: the nectar of flower

Nalakini: numerous lotuses; a lotus lake

Nalapriya: the beloved of king Nala; another name for Damayanti

Nalini: the lotus, numerous lotuses; aromatic beautiful; holy; dear to gods

Namita: bowed; bent down; meek

Namuchi: Kama; tight; permanent

Namya: to be bowed; the night

Nanda: Durga; happiness; joyful; prosperous

Nandana: happy; joyous; a name for Durga

Nandanti: happiness; a daughter

Nandi: happiness; a name for Durga

Nandika: one who gives pleasure; Indra's pleasure ground

Nandini: Durga; happy; a daughter

Nandita: one who pleases

Nandyanti: one who gives joy

Naomi: friend of Ruth; affable; beautiful

Narayani: Durga, Lakshmi; belonging to Vishnu or Krishna

Naristha: dear to woman; the Arabian jasmine

Narmada: one who gives pleasure

Natania: a feminine form of Nathan; gift of God

Navami: the ninth day of the Lunar month

Navangi: a beautiful woman

Navika: novel; young; fresh

Navina: young

Navisthi: songs of appreciation; a hymn

Naviya: new, young

Navmallika: the new creeper

Navya: new

Nayaja: daughter of wisdom

Nayaja: daughter of wisdom

Nayantara: star of one's eye; dear

Neha: loving; affectionate

Nibha: resembling; similar

Nichika: divided into parts; comprising all parts; a whole

Nichita: fully covered; a holy river of ancient India; another name for Ganga

Niddha: having a treasure; determined; bestowing, trying, striving

Nidhyana: intuition, sight

Nidhyati: meditation; reflection

Niharika: misty; the Milky Way

Nikriti: dishonesty; wickedness

Nilaksha: blue-eyed

Nilanjana: lightning

Nilima: blue

Nilimpika: a small cow

Nimisha: the twinkling of an eye

Nimrukti: sunset

Niraja: water-born; a pearl; a water lily

Nirajakshi: lotus-eyed; beautiful

Nirajita: enlightened

Niranjana: blemish-free; pure; clean; a name for Durga

Nirbha: to shine forth; appearance

Niriksha: not visible to the eye; anticipation

Nirmita: constructed

Nisha: clever, skilful

Nishama: unequalled

Nishika: honest; pure

Nishita: night

Nishtha: firmness; faith; determination

Nitika: a moral person; a leader

Nitya: Durga; immortal

Niyati: Durga; fate; destiny

Nripangana: belonging to a king; princess; queen

Nupur: an ornament worn on the toes; anklet

Nuriyah: another name for Hazrat Fatimah Zahra; lighted; resplendent; bright; shining

Nyayika: logician

Nyja: natural

Odati: rejuvenating; the dawn

Ohawna: God's gracious gift

Ojasvi: brave; resplendent; splendid

Ojasvini: brave; shining; energetic; powerful

Omala: the giver of *Om*; the holy word for the earth; giver of birth, life and death; the earth

Omisha: goddess of the sacred syllable Om; goddess of birth, life and death

Ondarya: generous; broadminded

Oorja: name of a sage's wife; power

Oormi: sea wave; a term in music

Oormika: sea wave; humming of a bee

Oorna: name of sage's wife

Oorvi: the earth

Oshadhi: medicine; medicinal herbs

P

Padma: Lakshmi; the lotus; the coloured one

Padmagriha: Lakshmi; one who resides in a lotus

Padmaja: Lakshmi; born of a lotus

Padmana: to one with a face like that of a lotus; a name for Lakshmi and Sarasvati

Padmanika: numerous lotuses

Padmanjali: an offering of lotuses

Padmarati: lover of lotuses

Padmarupa: one who has the beauty of a lotus; a name for Lakshmi

Padmini: lotus; a cluster of lotuses

Pakshalika: full of feathers

Pakshini: day of the full moon; a female bird

Palakshi: white

Palashini: covered with leaves; a river

Pallavi: blossoming; a young shoot Pallavika

Pallavika: looking like a blossom; a scarf

Panchali: princess of panchalas; a doll; friend of five; another name for Draupadi

Panishthi: admiration; appreciation

Panjari: impression of a full hand; a name for Narmada river

Pankajini: abounding in lotuses

Panya: appreciated; grand; eminent

Parama: that which is beyond physical world; the perfect woman

Paridhi: halo around the sun or the moon; a lamp or halo around the head of deities

Parinistha: one who is at the top of the summit; one who has complete knowledge

Parinita: complete; a married woman

Parivita: free; liked by everyone; the bow of Brahma

Parnasha: one who feeds on leaves; a river personified by an apsara of Varuna's court

Parnini: one with wings; leafy

Parokshi: beyond understanding; ambigious

Parthivi: daughter of the earth; another name for Sita or Lakshmi

Parul: practical; beautiful; charming

Parvani: the day of full moon

Parvini: a festival; holiday

Parvita: extremely free; liked by everybody; extremely useless

Pastya: house; goddess of household matters

Patali: the trumpet flower

Patangi: flying

Patangika: little bird; a little bee

Pathojini: a collection of lotus plants

Pathya: belonging to the path; way; road

Pauralika: pleasing; a *raga*

Pauravi: descended from Puru; a wife of Vasudeva; a wife of Yudhisthira; a *raga*

Pavaka: one who purifies; storm

Pavaki: purifying; the *Vedic* name of Sarasvati

Pavitra: pious; clean; beneficiant; sacred basil; a river

Pelava: delicate; fine; soft

Phalaya: flowers; buds

Philomena: a first century saint; love song; beloved

Pinakini: bow-shaped; one with a bow

Placidia: serene

Poloma: bow

Prabhati: the early morning song

Prachika: driving; a female falcon

Pradha: eminent; supreme

Pradhana: leader; most important; original;

Pradhi: very wise

Pragati: progress

Praharsha: happiness

Prajakta: mother of the people; goddess of creation

Prajna: intelligence; wisdom; a form of Sarasvati

Prajvala: lighted

Prakashika: one who enlightens; one who illuminates; famous

Prakhya: shining; mein; famous; celebrity

Prakriti: natural; nature personified as the Supreme Spirit

Pralambika: one that hangs down; a gold necklace; a pearl ornament

Prama: foundation

Pramika: best, greatest; one who fulfils desires

Pramiti: understanding; wisdom; prudence

Pramohini: attractive; infatuating

Pranati: bowing; offering to God

Pranayita: alive; bubbling with life

Pranita: led forward; conducted; progressed; written; composed

Praniti: conduct; guidance

Pranjati: upright; respectful

Pranyga: wisdom; safety; care

Prasaha: force; power; powerful

Prasami: peaceful; calm; tranquil

Prathana: prayer

Pratichya: from the west; one who is blessed with foresight

Pratika: symbolic; pretty; an image

Pratima: an image; likeness; symbol

Pratistha: stable; foundation; support

Prava: blowing forth

Pravara: best among women; a river of *Puranic* fame

Preksha: seeing; viewing

Prerita: one who is encouraged

Prerna: inspiration; direction

Prestha: dearest; most loved

Prishani: soft, mild, gentle

Prishti: a ray of light; touch

Prithika: jasmine

Priti: pleasure; joy; affection

Priyala: one who gives pleasure; a bunch of grapes

Puloma: one who is excited

Purala: Durga; guardian of fortresses

Puravi: belonging to the east; alive; a *ragini*

Puruvi: one who fulfils wishes; a *ragini*

Rachel: wife of Jacob; female sheep

Rachna: creation: production; achievement

Radhana: speech

Radhani: worship

Radhika: successful; prosperous; a name for
    Radha

Ragini: melody; love; elder sister of Parvati; a
    form of Lakshmi; a musical mode in
    Indian classical music

Rajani: Durga; night; queen; turmeric; the
    dusky one

Rajavi: royal bird

Rajini: a collection of blue lotuses

Rajita: enlightened; shining; bright; brilliant

Rakshita: guarded

Rakshita: guarded; an apsara who was the daughter of Kashyap and Pradha

Ramakiri: present everywhere; a *ragini*

Ramala: one who gives pleasure; a lover Ramana, Ramani, Ramanika

Ramana: attractive; worthy of being loved; gracious; endearing

Ramani: one who is worthy of being loved; happy; pleasure-giving; pretty; gracious

Ramanika: affectionate; happy, gay; beautiful

Ramayani: the mirror of Rama; one who is well-versed in the *Ramayana*

Rameshvari: consort of Rama

Ramila: one who gives pleasure; lover

Ramya: enchanting; attractive; appealing

Ranajita: victorious in battle

Ranhita: efficient; quick

Ranjana: pleasing; exciting; charming

Ranvita: happy, delightful

Ranya: pleasant

Raphaela: one of the four archangels; healed by God

Rasana: one who knows the taste; the tongue; taste; understanding

Rasanika: a ray of light

Rasanjma: one who is aware of sentiments; full of sentiments

Rashmika: a tiny ray of light

Rashtri: ruler

Rasika: one who is tasteful; elegant; gracious

Rasya: emotional; full of feelings

Rathya: crossroads; a group of chariots

Ratija: daughter of the truth

Ratnolka: a jewelled nectar

Ratrika: the night

Raupya: one that is made of silver, a *Puranic* river in ancient India

Ravishta: loved by the sun

Raziyah: another name for Hazrat Fatimah Zahra; joyous; contented

Rebecal: the wife of Isaac; tied; bound

Rebha: one who sings praises

Reva: agile, quick; wife of Karna; another name for Narmada and Kali

Revati: flourishing; wealth

Ribhya: worshipped

Riddhi: prosperity, wealth, abundance; superiority; one of the wives of Ganesha; another name for Lakshmi and Parvati

Riddhima: auspicious; prosperous; the season of spring; love

Rina: dissolved

Rishma: moonbeam

Rishva: ascending; high; noble

Rista: sword; another name for the mother of apsaras

Ritika: belonging to a stream; brass

Ritu: time period

Ritushri: queen of seasons

Riya: one who sings

Rochana: bright; resplendent; good-looking woman

Rohini: rising; increasing; tall

Roma: full of hair

Romala: hairy; charming

Romasha: one who has thick hair

Roshansha: longing, desire

Royina: ascending; growing

Ruchi: beauty; interest; lustre; light

Ruchika: shining; interesting; desirable

Ruchira: desirable; affable; pleasing

Ruchita: resplendent; sweet, bright

Rudhi: ascending; birth; illustrious

Rudra: Parvati, consort of Shiva; crying

Rudrani: Parvati; the wife of Rudra; a form of Shiva emerged from Brahma's eyebrows

Ruhika: one who ascends; wish

Rupali: one with a beautiful form

Rupangi: one with a beautiful body

Rupasi: beautiful

Rupika: one who has a beautiful body, appearance; coin of gold and silver

Ruqayyah: ascending; height; daughter of Prophet Muhammad and Hazrat Khadijah

Rushati: white; fair-complexioned

Ruth: friend of Naomi; companionship

S

Saachika: truthful

Sachi: air; kindness; generosity

Sadhaka: Durga; swift; active; fertile; fantastical

Sadhana: achievement; worship

Sadhvi: virtuous; noble; chaste

Sadhya: achievement; perfection

Sagarika: belonging to the ocean

Sahima: covered with snow

Sahita: proximity; a river

Sahitra: enduring

Sakshi: witness

Salome: calm; sister of King Herod

Saloni: beautiful

Sama: peaceful; tranquil; equanimity; a year

Samajya: illustrious, famous

Samali: a bouquet of flowers

Samani: calm, peaceful

Samata: equality; peaceful

Samawiyah: another name for Hazrat
Fatimah Zahra; heavenly; light breeze

Samedhi: moving one

Samichi: appreciation; eulogy; a doe; an
apsara

Samiha: longing, desire

Samisha: dart

Sampangi: one who has a balanced body

Sampriti: complete satisfaction; joy; delight

Sampriya: fully loved; dear; beloved

Samriti: meeting

Samroddhi: prosperty; flourishing; wealth

Sanah: radiant; bright; resplendent

Sananda: a form of Lakshmi; delightful; gay; full of pleasure

Sandhya: dusk

Sangani: companion

Sanitra: gift; an offering to gods

Sanjali: with hands hollowed and joined in prayer

Sanjanya: merciful, generous; loving; friendly; compassionate

Sanjiti: one who is victorious

Sanjogita: attached; joined together

Sannati: bowing, modesty; humble

Sanoja: immortal

Sanoli: analytical

Sanrakta: full of blood, red-coloured

Santusti: complete satisfaction

Sanuritti: existing; becoming; happening

Sanvitti: wisdom; intellect; harmony

Sanyakta; joined together; united

Saparya: worship; admiration

Saprya: worship; homage

Sara: fixed; hard; valuable; best

Sarah: wife of Abraham; mother of Isaac;
    princess

Sarangi: a spotted doe

Saranya: one who protects; one who gives
    shelter; another name for Durga

Sargini: made of parts

Sarika: a form of Durga; the Mynah bird;
    confident

Sarupa: similar; good-looking

Sarvajina: Durga; one who knows
    everything; universal

Sarvani: Durga; universal; complete

Sarveshi: wanted by all

Sarvika: universal; whole

Sarvika: universal; complete, whole

Sashrika: one who is endowed with beauty; grace; fortune

Sashthi: Durga; appreciation; a hymn

Sattviki: Durga; true; pure; honest

Saumya: Durga; related to the moon; peaceful; pleasant; mild; a pearl

Sauvarna: made of gold

Sauviri: daughter of a hero

Savini: one who gives nectar; a river

Sayyidah: another name for Hazrat Fatimah, descendant of the Holy Prophet; woman; head

Serafina: Seraphim are the highest order of angles; fiery; hot

Shaila: residing in the mountains; Parvati's mother

Shailasha: Parvati; one who lives in the mountain

Shaili: style; habit; custom

Shailja: Parvati; daughter of the mountain

Shaini: prosperity; another name for Goddess Mansa

Shakerni: lucky object; a good omen

Shakivi: Parvati; goddess of herbs; powerful

Shakunika: bird
Shakuntala, Shakunti, Shakuntika

Shakuntala: bird; guarded by birds

Shakunti: bird

Shakuntika: a small bird

Shalika: flute

Shalina: courteous; fennel

Shalini: one who has a fixed abode; settled; bashful; modest

Shamani: pacifier; night

Shamasti: accomplishing; whole; the universe

Shamika: peaceful

Shamika: tranquil

Shamira: the chameli flower

Shankaharini: one that possesses branches best

Shankalika: without any faults

Shansita: desired; appreciated; famous

Shansita: wished; desired for

Shantina: bearer of peace; affable; kind

Sharada: Durga; a lute bearer

Sharadi: autumn; modest

Sharadika: belonging to the autumn

Sharani: the earth; protector; guardian

Sharmistha: the lucky one; wife of Yayati

Sharvari: night

Shasti: praise

Shastika: a form of Durga supposed

Shatakshi: Durga; the night; 100-eyed

Sheralini: one who has moss-like surface; a river

Shivani: Parvati; the wife of Shiva

Shivika: palanquin

Shreya: most beautiful; best

Shrila: granted by Lakshmi; auspicious; prosperous; joyful; famous

Shubhya: auspicious

Shuchika: pious, holy; an aspara

Sidhiksha: Lakshmi; a religious ceremony

Sirina: night

Smera: smiling; affable; evident

Snakriti: good-looking

Snigdha: soft; affable; brilliant; charming; graceful

Somali: deer to the moon

Sonakshi: Parvati; golden-eyed

Spandana: heartbeat; very beautiful

Srinjayi: granter of victory

Sriti: path, road

Sthira: determined; another name for the
    earth

Striratna: Lakshmi; jewel of a woman

Stuti: invocation

Suchita: favourable; pious

Sudena: Lakshmi; a real goddess

Sudiksha: another name for Lakshmi

Suhela: easily approachable

Sukala: a good part; very talented

Sukanya: a pretty girl

Sukriti: benevolent, generous; auspicious

Suloma: one with beautiful hair; Indian
    redwood

Sumantika: the Indian white rose

Sumaya: well-planned; a daughter of Maya

Sunaya: just; well-behaved; the mother of a
Jain Tiranthankara

Sunayana: one with beautiful eyes

Sundhuja: Lakshmi; born of the ocean

Suniksha: one with beautiful ornaments

Suparna: Parvati; leaves; a lotus plant

Surana: happy, delightful; making a pleasing
sound; a river

Surasa: Durga; well-flavoured; affectionate;
graceful

Surmya: good-looking

Suryani: wife of the sun

Suvali: graceful, elegant

Suvena: with a beautiful braid; *Puranic* river
which sage Markandeya saw in the
stomach of the child Krishna

Sveni: white

Tahirah: another name for Hazrat Fatimah
Zahra; pure; virtuous

Talakhya: fragrance; the scent of a palm
tree

Talika: the palm; nightingale

Talinodari: one with a small waist

Taluni: a young girl

Tama: night

Tamaharini: one who removes darkness; a
deity who destroys darkness

Tamasa: one who is dark-coloured; a river that merges with the Ganga and on whose banks was the ashrama of Valmiki

Tamasi: night; slumber; a river; a name for Durga Tamasvini, Tami

Tamasvini: night

Tami: night

Tamra: copper-crested

Tamrakarni: copper - eared

Tamrika: copperish

Tanishi: might, strength, bravery; a daughter of Indra; another name for the earth

Tanubhava: daughter

Tanuja: born of the body; a daughter

Tanushri:: one with a heavenly body

Tanuvi· a fragile woman
Tanvi

Tanvangi: slender-limbed

Tanvi: fragile; pretty

Tapani: heat; a river

Tapanti: healing; a river

Tapati: belonging to the river Tapati

Tapi: warmth; radiance; a name for Tapati river

Tapsvini: an ascetic

Tapushi: a burning weapon

Taraka: star, falling star, meteor; the eye; Brihaspati's wife

Tarakini: starry; night

Tarana: a song

Tarika: one who belongs to the stars

Tarini: Durga; one who helps to cross over

Tarita: Durga; the forefinger; the leader

Tarpini: satisfying; offerings made to the God

Taruni: a young girl

Tarushi: victory

Tatripi: intensely satisfying

Tavara Parni: one with red leaves

Tayyibah: another name for Hazrat Fatimah
    Zahra; another name for the city of
    Medina; holy; virtuous

Tejashri: one who has divine powers

Tejini: sharp; bright; active

Tilaka: a type of necklace

Tilika: a small mark of sandalwood

Timila: a musical instrument

Tirtha: path; a place of pilgrimage

Titiksa: patience to protect children

Talakshi: with green eyes

Toshani: Durga; contented; pleasing

Toyanive: the earth

Trarita: Durga; agile; efficient, swift

Trayi: wisdom; comprehension; the three *Vedas*

Treya: one who walks in three paths

Tridhara: one with three streams; a name for river Ganga

Trigarta: heaven

Trijagati: Parvati; mother of the three worlds

Tripti: satisfaction, water

Tripura: Durga; a kind of cardamom

Trishala: the mother of Mahavira

Trishna: thirst; daughter of Kama

Triveni: the meeting of the three rivers Ganga, Yamuna and Sarasvati

Triya: young woman

Truti: an atom; a moment of time

Tulini: the cotton tree

Turya: one who possesses power

Tushita: contented

Tvesha: shining, bright
    Tvishi

Tvisha: bright; shining; resplendent

Tvishi: shining; bright

Uchchata: height; excellence

Udantika: protected; contented

Udayanti: ascending; eminent; good

Udbhuti: appearing; existence

Udgiti: singing

Uditi: the sunrise

Udu: water

Udvaha: continuation; a daughter

Udvahni: glowing; shining

Udyati: height; ascending

Ugrakarnika: one with large earrings

Ujjayati: one who has won; victorious

Ujjesha: victorious

Ujjiti: victory

Ujjvala: bright; clean

Ujjvalita: lighted; shining; brilliant

Uktharka: a hymn recited in the praise of the sun

Ukti: proclamation; speech

Ulkushi: a meteor

Uluki: a she owl

Ulupi: one with an attractive face

Uma: Parvati born as daughter of Himavat and Mena

Unmada: one who is very beautiful

Unmadini: very attractive

Unmukti: deliverance

Unnati: flourishing; advance, dignity; ascending; the wife of Garuda; a daughter of Daksha and wife of Dharma

Upadhriti: a ray of light

Upakarika: one who protects

Upama: resembalance; similarity

Upanayika: fit for an offering

Upaniti: initiation

Upasti: admiration; worship

Urja: Parvati; energy, strength, vitality; food; water; breath

Urjal: active; strength; food; water; breath; another name for Parvati

Urjani: belonging to energy; daughter of the sun; goddess of strength

Urjjasvati: full of energy; vigorous

Urmi: wave, ripple, light
Urmika, Urmila, Urmya

Urmika: seawave; ring finger; humming of bees

Urmila: waves of passion; pretty; magical

Urmya: path; night; *Vedic* goddess of light

Urna: woollen

Urusha: one who produces amply

Uruta: greatness

Urvara: fertile soil; the earth

Urvashi: extends vastly

Urvi: the earth; the heaven and earth together

Ushana: longing; desire

Ushi: desire; longing

Ushija: born of a desire, longing; active; enthusiastic; beautiful

Uti: wish

Utkalika: one who desires to be famous; a bud; a wave

Utkanika: wish, desire

Utkanti: splendour

Utkarika: composed of precious material; made of milk and ghee

Utkarthini: fulfilling one's ambitions

Utkhala: perfume

Utkuja: the cooing note of the Kokila

Utpalakshi: Lakshmi; lotus-eyed; a goddess

Utpalini: a collection of lotuses

Uttamika: best worker

Uttara: the northern direction

Uttarika: crossing over; delivering; a boat; a river

Uttejini: animated; excited

Uttejini: exciting

V

Vacha: speech

Vachya: Sita

Vagishvari: goddess of speech

Vahini: an army; body of force

Vahyaka: chariot

Vaibhavi: strength; grandeur

Vaidagdhi: grace; beauty

Vaidarbhi: coming from Vidarbha

Vaidehi: princess of the Videhas; another
name for Sita

Vaidhriti: one with a similar disposition

Vaijayantika: one who gives victory; banner; pearl necklace

Vaikuntha: without any obstacles; abode of the absolute

Vaimitra: a friend of the universe

Vainavi: belonging to Venu; gold from the Venu river

Vairagi: free from passions

Vairawi: wife of Daksha

Vaisakhi: the day of the full moon in the month of *Vaisakh*

Vaishalini: daughter of the great; the daughter of King Vishal

Vaishnavi: worshipper of Vishnu

Vaitarini: one who crosses the physical world; one who helps in crossing the physical world; a river which flows in Orissa

Vaivasvati: belonging to the sun

Vajra: Durga; powerful; courageous

Vaksana: one who nourishes the river bed; rejuvenation; offering to god; fire Vakshani, Vaksi

Vakshani: one who strengthens

Vaksi: night; nourishment; fire

Vallabha: dear

Vallaki: a lute

Vallari: a cluster of flowers; a creeper; a name for Sita

Vallika: enveloped with vines; greenery

Valoguki: very beautiful

Vama: a form of Durga; Lakshmi, Sarasvati; beautiful

Vamakshi: beautiful-eyed

Vamana: small; an apsara

Vamani: bringer of wealth; small

Vamanika: small; tiny

Vamika: situated on the left side; another name for Durga

Vanaja: born of a forest

Vanalika: belonging to the forest; sunflower

Vanathi: belonging to the forest

Vancha: longing; wish

Vandana: prayer; worship

Vandinika: appreciated; revered Vandita, Vandya

Vandita: appreciated; revered

Vandya: one who is worth appreciating; adorable

Vani: Sarasvati; speech; appreciation; melodious voice

Vanya: belonging to the wood; rosary pea

Vara: Parvati; blessing; gift; precious

Varalika: Durga; goddess of power; the chief of the army

Varangi: having a beautiful body

Varasya: longing; desire

Varenya: wanted by everyone; Shiva's wife

Varisha: the monsoon season

Varnika: of a good colour; gold

Varunani: the goddess of water

Varuthini: an army

Vasantika: goddess of spring

Vasati: dawn

Vasudha: Lakshmi; the earth; one who produces

Vasundhareyi: Sita; daughter of the earth

Vasura: valuable

Vasvi: divine night

Vatsa: daughter

Vatya: storm

Vawalika: belonging to a forest

Vaya: twig; a child

Vayodha: strengthening

Venika: constantly flowing; a holy river of the *Puranas*

Venya: wished for

Vidipita: lighted

Viha: heaven

Vilashini: shining, bright; another name for Lakshmi

Vinayika: the consort of Ganesha

Virani: brave woman; a daughter of Brahma born from his left thumb

Virika: brave

Virya: strength; active

Vishalakshi: Durga; one with long eyes

Vishruti: famous

Vitasta: the measure of length from the
wrist to the tip of the fingers

Vyusti: first ray of dawn; beautiful;
reward; happiness

Wabisah: lightning

Wadifat: a green meadow

Wafa: faithfulness

Wafrah: ample; plenty; abundance

Wahaf: blossom

Waheeda: beautiful

Wahidah: unique

Wahilah: Prophet Noah's wife who was an
    unbeliever

Waiyah: a fine pearl

Wajnah: check

Walidaha: daughter, young girl

Wamika: goddess

Wamil: beautiful

Wana: turtle dove

Wanat: pearl

Wanyat: a string of pearls

Warisat: heiress

Wasimah: good-looking, pretty

Wishnah: black cherry

Wushah: a belt set in jewels worn by ladies

Yael : strength of God

Yahua: the heaven and the earth

Yajnika: used in offering to the gods

Yakshangi: a river; alive; swift

Yamala: a river

Yamini: night

Yamya: night

Yastika: a string of pearls

Yati: patient, endurance

Yogita: attractive; magical; wild

Yoshana: girl, a young woman
Yosita: woman, wife
Yubhika: numerous

Zabu: female hyena

Zacharie: remembering God

Zafum: female dancer

Zaha: beautiful flower; blossom; radiance,
    shining

Zahab: golden

Zahanat: wisdom; prudence

Zaharah: spirit; fresh; strength

Zahat: eye

Zahidah: abstinent; pious

Zahirah: flower

Zahra: Prophet Muhammad's daughter; good-looking; fair; calm; gracious

Zahrah: flower; beautiful

Zakiyah: another name for Hazrat Fatimah Zahra; clean; chaste; truthful; wise

Zamran: sweet basil

Zarenya: golden

Zarin: golden

Zaritah: pretty; charming

Zeba: decorated; beautiful; graceful

Zebunisha: an ornament among women; daughter of Emperor Aurangzeb

Zeenat: fame

Zewar: jewellery

Ziba: female hyenas

Zilpha: Jacob's wife; stately; noble

Zipporah: Moses' wife; bird

Zohra: the planet Jupiter

Zubaidah: butter: wife of Khalifah Harun at Rashid who is said to have narrated the stories of the Arabian nights

Zubarah: flower; the planet venus

Zulekha: beautiful

Zurahinah: faultless girl

Zurlah: flower; beautiful, fair; pretty; glowing

Zusha: bracelet

Zuwabah: ringlet; curd